Table of Contents

Spanakopita/Tiropites filo/puff

Sikotakia

Avgolemono

Fakies

Fassolada

Fava

Keftedakia

Dolmathes

Saganaki

Pastitsio

Mousaka

Psomi

Thank you

Introduction

A normal diet for many Americans is largely comprised of red meat, animal fats and preservatives. As most of us do not eat home cooked meals our busy lifestyles force us to eat out. Actually, hardly will you find an easy to make diet that is rich in veggies and fruits, which means that we never provide our bodies with essential anti-oxidants, vitamins and other nutrients that help keep our bodies healthy and free from illness.

Obviously, the human body is not built to digest processed food and as much red meat as we consume. The foods we buy prepared for us probably contain substances that humans have not yet started digesting and absorbing. This has in turn weakened the immune system, which subsequently brings many chronic illnesses that were rare in the past.

Most of us know the Mediterranean diet is rich in veggies and fruits and provides a wide range of benefits to our general health. However, eating fish and seafood is recommended twice a week. For instance, following a Mediterranean diet will significantly reduce health complications like cancer, high blood pressure, type 2 diabetes, Alzheimer's, obesity and disease. So, what does a Mediterranean diet refer to and entail?

In a nutshell, a Mediterranean diet describes the common diet that originated from countries around the Mediterranean. One of the biggest contributors of high blood pressure is the excessive emphasis on salt in meals especially in the normal Western diet. When you adopt a Mediterranean diet you consume more of herbs to reduce the reliance on salt. This isn't really a diet but a lifestyle whereby you start eating healthy everyday of your life by:

- Increasing your intake of veggies, legumes, wholegrain cereals and fruits.

- Reducing or control your consumption of red meat and replacing it with fish and poultry.

- Reducing or control your consumption of processed foods, ready foods and fast foods since these are often high in fat and salt.

- Starting to eat more limited amounts of dairy products that are low in fat.

- Cooking using mono-unsaturated oils like olive oil

- Snacking on fruits, unsalted nuts and veggies as opposed to cakes, biscuits and crisps

- Taking red wine during meals and limiting consumption to 2 small glasses daily

- Taking plenty of water.

In addition to, one should avoid these foods:

- Added sugar: sodas, ice cream, table sugar , candies and many more

- Refried grain: white bread, flour, rice and many more

- Trans fat: the use of margarine and many of the processed food

- Refined oils: canola oil, sunflower oil, cottonseed oil, and many others

- Processed meats: hotdogs, sausages, canned meats and many others

We cannot go through a Greek cookbook without mentioning the beautiful country of Greece. Greece (Hellas) is one of the oldest nations in the world. It has a unique culture and civilization with a long, interesting history. Greece's history has several historical phases through war and migration that has made the finest gourmet food and the finest wines with each region offering different specialties. Hellenic food is famous for its world wide array of delicious delicacies. Some of the food today was eaten in ancient times as historians have discovered that food such as dolmathes, fruits, and grains were eaten by their ancestors. Additionally, Greece is an Orthodox Christian nation and many Greeks follow the traditions of the church. On certain days, they either eat no meat, fish, dairy, or no food at all. There are strict dietary rules for lent, holy week, and most Wednesdays and Fridays. After these days are respected, Greeks are known for their extravagant feasts. Greeks love their fish and seafood as the country is surrounded by water. The healthiest type of dairy product is goat cheese as it contains the least amount of lactose compared to cow's milk. Goat's milk also has the least amount of fat and cholesterol which in turn makes it easier to digest. In addition to this, goat's milk contains fewer harmful substances. It is high in vitamin K, D, thiamine, niacin, vitamin B riboflavin, and mineral phosphorous. The body cannot create minerals and vitamins on its own so goat cheese provides this for our body. The Mediterranean diet has shown that it is the world's healthiest diet. For example the island of Ikaria is known to have the longest life expectancy of any other place on earth. People from the island stick to this diet and live on average well into their 90's. Their lifestyle promotes the Mediterranean diet with olive oil, goat cheese, unsalted food and delicious wines with long walks near the ocean allowing these Greeks to have the greatest longevity in the world. You will never see a Greek man within the country and abroad eat fast food, canned food or processed food.

This book will discuss how to make 25 Greek appetizers to help you adopt the Mediterranean diet easily; you will be amazed by how delicious these appetizers will be to make and enjoy.

Greek Salad

Makes 6 servings

Ingredients

1 finely sliced red onion

- 1 chopped, dried and rinsed head romaine lettuce.
- 1 Whole black olive, Kalamata if you can get them!
- 1 finely chopped red bell pepper
- 1 finely chopped green bell pepper
- 1 cup feta cheese (crumbled)
  2 well chopped large tomatoes
- 1 sliced cucumber
- 1 teaspoon oregano (dry)
- 6 tablespoons olive oil
- Ground black pepper

Directions

1. Using a peeler take off 4 strips of the skin on the cucumber if it's a thick

skin. Cut the ends off the cucumber then quarter the cucumber lengthwise. Cut the cucumber into 15mm chunks and set aside.

2. Core the stems off the tomatoes (the white not so tasty part) and then cut in half, then cut each half into 6 chunks and put aside. Do not mix the tomatoes and cucumbers together right away as the acid in the tomato will ruin the cucumber a little especially if you're putting this in the fridge while you prepare other meals. I personally cut the tomato and onion last.

3. Cut the onions down the middle and then start at one end so that you get thin slices. Thick chunks of onion in one bite are not appealing, so break them apart. You want to end up with thin crescent shape onion slices not chunks, also because of the chemical make-up of the onion you want to put these aside and combine right before serving.

4. Core the peppers rinsing out the seeds then try cutting them skin facing up (a lot easier this way than having to slice through the skin every time) into 5mm x 20-40mm strips.

5. Take only the feta you will use out of the brine you bought it in with a clean knife. When putting back feta into the brine again, it possibly leads to an increase of bacteria which will ruin the taste in future uses. Crumble the feta in your fists under a plate or blade whichever you prefer and mix in a little oregano.

6. Now for the important part, preparing and serving. Get your bowl and drop in the ingredients in this order; tomato, onion, some feta, some oregano, some olive oil, black pepper, cucumber the remainder of the feta and oregano, and olives. Then drizzle with olive oil and serve. Opa!

Notes: pick a sharper solid feta, there are some variations of feta out there which aren't authentic, for instance Bulgarian feta has the consistency of cottage cheese. This could be used if it is your thing but it lacks the salt and taste of the Greek feta.

Other common ingredients you can add are:

- Lemon juice

- Balsamic vinegar

- Dill

- Capers

Tzatziki

Makes 6 Servings

Ingredients

- 1 drained, grated and finely seeded English cucumber
- 1 liter of plain yogurt
- 2 minced cloves garlic
- 2 tablespoons of fresh dill (chopped)
- Freshly cracked white pepper with sea salt
- Cheese cloth

Directions

1. Take the garlic cloves and place in a food processor with some oil and blend it into a paste. If you do not have a processor, you can use a knife and repeatedly chop the garlic into very small pieces.

2. Take the cheese cloth and set it down on a clean counter and place all of

the yogurt in the middle of the cloth. Fold the cloth up and hang the cloth over the sink and let the water strain out. This will take 1/2hr or more depending on how thick and creamy you want it. I would let it stand overnight in the refrigerator. Remember the longer you let it stand the less yogurt will remain.

3. Add the strained yogurt to a serving bowl.

4. Grate the cucumber and remove as much of the moisture out of it as you can by wringing it in the cheese cloth.

5. Place the cucumber and the garlic in the serving bowl with the yogurt and mix.

6. Add oil and white pepper then mix.

7. Add some salt and pepper to taste. Top with dill and an olive if you wish. Serve with hot pita bread and some Ouzo! Opa!

You can add some more garlic and white pepper for the extra kick. Do it! Put some hair on your chest. Did you think all that hair is a genetic trait? Opa Opa Opa!!!

Tirokafteri *(Spicy Greek Feta Dip)*

Makes 4 servings

Ingredients

- 250g of cubed Greek feta

- 1-tablespoon of extra-virgin olive oil

- 1 teaspoon of Tabasco to taste

- ½ teaspoon of wild oregano (dry)

- 1 Whole red pepper

- Handful of basil or parsley as a garnish

Directions

1. Put all the ingredients in a food processor.

2. Process until smooth and serve garnished with chopped parsley.

3. Serve with pita and enjoy with some wine and good company. I know what you're thinking; this can't be it, that's it. You could always break a plate on the floor, Opa!

Mint/feta dip

Makes 3 to 4 Servings

Ingredients

- 250 grams of feta cheese (crumbled) 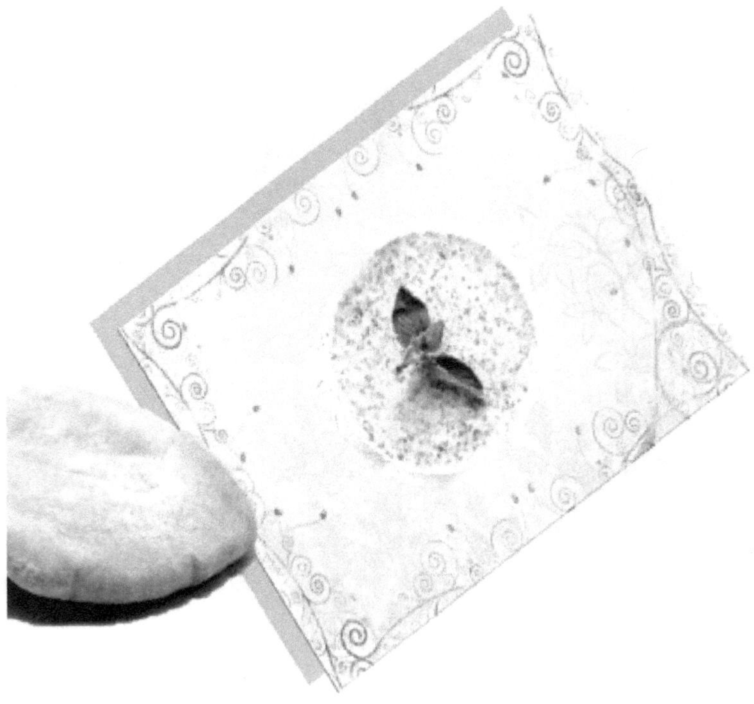
- 1 handful well chopped mint leaves
- 1/8 cup of olive oil
- Parsley

Directions

1. Crumble the feta cheese using your hands or cut into small chunks to be blended in a food processor.

2. Place the chopped mint leaves and the feta into a food processor.

3. Firstly, add the olive oil while blending while very slowly.

4. Then as needed add water to help break up the feta. Eventually, there should be enough water to create the desired consistency. Keep blending until very smooth.

5. If you like, you can add some salt to taste but the cheese might already have more than enough. Garnish with parsley and serve with pita. Opa!

Olive Pati

Makes 4 servings

Ingredients

- 1 cup of small pitted Calamata olives
- 1/8 cup of drained oven-dried tomatoes
- 1 garlic clove
- 1/8 cup of extra-virgin olive oil
- 1 slice of pita

Directions

1. Set aside the olive oil and combine all ingredients in a food processor. Use pulse mode to process into a smooth spread.

2. Slowly add olive oil and pieces of bread while continuing to process.

3. Cover and refrigerate for a few hours then serve chilled. Opa!

Skordalia

Makes 3 Cups

Ingredients

- 12 minced medium cloves garlic

- 2 slices of pita bread

- 1/4 cup of extra-virgin olive oil

- 5 tablespoons of lemon juice (freshly squeezed)

- ½ cup of water

- kosher salt

- Dill as garnish

Directions

1. Take garlic and blend with the oil in a food processor.

2. Add the bread and continue to process into a paste.

3. Add water slowly until desired consistency is reached.

4. Add salt and lemon juice to taste.

5. Garnish with dill and possibly an olive, and don't forget the Opa!

Taramosalata

Makes 6 Servings

Ingredients

- 4 ounces of tarama
- 4 slices of dry bread
- 1 medium sized onion
- 1/8 cup of olive oil
- 1/4 cup lemon juice
- Salt and pepper

Directions:

1. Soak dried bread in water then wring dry.
   In a food processor, blend bread, tarama, and onion until the mixture is smooth while adding lemon juice to taste.
2. Slowly add olive oil checking the consistency and flavor as you go.
3. Then serve in a bowl with some pita bread.
4. Finally, garnish with either parsley and/or olive. Opa!

Homous - *creamy dip or spread made from white chickpeas*

Make 5 servings

Ingredients

- ½ cup of white sesame seeds (roasted and powdered) or ½ cup tahini

- ½ cup of olive oil

- 1 1/2 cup of soaked and cooked chickpeas

- ½-teaspoon of cayenne pepper or red chili powder

- 3 garlic cloves

- Few sprigs of coriander/cilantro or parsley

- Salt to taste

- 1-teaspoon of cumin powder

Directions:

1. Place the chick peas in a food processor. Blend the chick peas with the

olive oil until you get a smooth paste. You want to end up with a paste that has very little or no large chunks.

2. At this point, add the tahini and the garlic and continue blending until absolutely no solids remain.

3. Adding the cayenne and cumin, blend well while slowly adding salt to taste.

4. Chop the parsley/cilantro into fine pieces and sprinkle over top.

5. Serve with pita bread or celery. Opa? Celery? Really? Actually that's pretty good… Opa!

Melitzanosalata

Makes 8 servings

Ingredients

- 125 ml or half cup of olive oil
- 1 crushed clove garlic finely chopped
- 4 large purple eggplants
- 4 tablespoons of lemon juice
- 1/2 red onion finely chopped
- 3 tablespoons of chopped fresh parsley
- Sea salt to taste
- Freshly ground pepper

Directions:

1. Cut the eggplants into halves.

2. Prepare a baking tray lined with parchment paper and place the eggplant halves on it.

3. Coat the eggplant halves with olive oil and then season with pepper and salt.

4. Sprinkle fresh thyme and two finely chopped cloves of garlic over top.

5. Preheat oven to 200F.

6. Cover with another baking tray and bake for 20 minutes.

7. When finished cooking, remove from the oven and scrape the inner pulp out of the eggplant halves into a bowl.

8. With a wooden spoon, thoroughly mix the lemon juice.

9. Add salt and pepper to taste.

10. Let the mixture cool down and refrigerate in order to incorporate flavors.

11. Top with a black olive and serve with pita bread. Opa!

Delicious Beet Salad

Makes 4 Servings

Ingredients

- 3 tablespoon of dill (finely chopped)

- 1-bunch of beets

- 2-tablespoon of balsamic vinegar

- 1/4 teaspoon of salt

- 3-tablespoon of olive oil

Directions:

1. Trim green tops from beets. Place the greens aside.

2. Wash the beets thoroughly and place in a pan. Fill with water then bring to a boil over high.

3. Reduce heat to medium, cover the pan partially and boil gently for 30 minutes.

4. Rinse and drain in cool water then peel and slice into six slices.

5. Whisk vinegar, salt, oil and dill in a bowl.

6. After washing, pat dry beet greens then chop coarsely and combine all the ingredients. Toss and serve.

7. Warning: Kids may not like this but it is really good for you. Opa!

Horta - Boiled Green Leafy Vegetables

Makes 4 Servings

Ingredients

- ½ pounds of endives or your choice of dark leafy greens

- Sea salt

- Freshly ground pepper

- Extra virgin olive oil

- 2 lemons

Directions:

1. Wash the greens.

2. Remove the damaged leaves and stems.

3. Place the endives into a pot and then cover with water.

4. Boil for 15 minutes.

5. Drain out and mix 3 tablespoons of olive oil along with two tablespoons of lemon juice, pepper and salt.

6. Serve hot or cold if you like.

7. Add a piece of feta on the side for extra appeal.

This is the answer of the Greek population to the hunger brought on by the German occupation. What do you do when the animals you used to get your milk from are no longer anywhere to be found. All you have is the grass the animals used to eat which are mostly weeds and grass but edible and nutritious. But then after the war you keep eating it? Us offspring of our Greek parents who survived the war never understood this. Mmmm! Boiled grass (literal translation from Greek). Opa!

Grilled Kalamari - *Kalamari tis Skaras*

Makes 6 servings

Ingredients

- 5 tablespoons of olive oil

- 1/2 pounds of whole squid

- 1 teaspoon of oregano (dry)

- 2 cloves finely minced garlic

- 1/2 teaspoon of salt

- Lemon juice

- Fresh squeezed lemon for serving

- 1/4 teaspoon of black pepper (freshly ground)

- 1 teaspoon of baking soda

- 1/8 pound of unsalted butter

Directions:

1. Prepare the kalamari by removing the outer skin and gutting out the intestines and small bone which looks like a long thin piece of clear plastic.

2. Combine garlic, olive oil, oregano, baking soda, pepper and salt in a large bowl then add the pieces of kalamari and toss to coat.

3. Cover the bowl and place it into a refrigerator for half an hour.

4. Take the prepared kalamari out of the refrigerator and put it on the grill.

5. Grill over medium high heat without letting the kalamari dry out or burn.

6. Periodically take the kalamari off the grill and rinse off any black residue with butter. Place more butter inside the kalamari and continue barbequing. Repeating these steps keeps the kalamari moist and cools it enough so it does not burn. Do not allow the open flame to touch the

kalamari for too long.

7. Once cooked, pour lemon juice over top, and serve with some Tzatziki.
    Opa!

Garides Skaras

Makes 6 Servings

Ingredients

- 10 pureed garlic cloves
- 36 green prawns
- 2 cups of canola oil
- 1/4 cups butter
- 1 teaspoon of salt
- 2 teaspoons of pepper
- 1 teaspoon baking soda

Directions:

1. Take the prawns and place them in a bowl.

2. Set up a cutting board and a small sharp knife. Gripping the prawn from the tail, put your other finger under the scale of the prawn near the legs and pull it away working your way up to the head. Leave the tail on as a handle when eating as finger food.

3. Take each prawn and make a slit across its back about 1-3mm deep so you can pull out the intestine and discard.

4. Rinse the prawn with clean water and place in another clean bucket or bowl containing ice water.

5. Using a bamboo skewer about 10" long place 6 prawns on each skewer piercing the prawn in through the back and again out through the back as per the diagram below.

6. Mix the pureed garlic, canola oil, baking soda, salt and pepper in a container.

7. Melt the butter and then pour and mix it into the oil.

8. Place the prawn skewers in the marinade and turn to coat.

9. Put the completed skewers in the refrigerator for half an hour to 24 hours.

10. Preheat barbeque to moderate and place prawn skewers on to cook. Only flip them when they cook halfway through. You want the middle to just start to cook through when you remove them from heat. Overcooking the prawn will make it taste dry.

11. Finally, with the finished product, you brush well with an oil/butter/lemon juice mixture.

12. Put onto a serving platter and garnish with lemon and parsley. Enjoy, Opa!.

Spanakopites/Tiropites - *with puff pastry and filo pastry*

Makes 6 Servings

Ingredients

- 1 large beaten egg with 1 tablespoon of water 

- 3 tablespoons of butter (unsalted)

- 3 finely chopped garlic cloves

- 1/2 teaspoon of nutmeg

- 2 chopped medium onions

- 2 boxes of squeezed and thawed frozen chopped spinach

- 3/4 cup of grated parmesan cheese

- 1 cup of crumbled feta cheese

- 4 beaten extra-large eggs

- 1-teaspoon of salt

- 2 sheets of filo or puff pastry (frozen)

- 3/4 teaspoon of white pepper

- Sesame seeds (optional)

Directions:

1. Preheat oven to 375 deg. F.

2. Line a baking sheet with parchment paper.

3. Melt butter in a saucepan.

4. Add the onions to the butter and cook onions until soft.

5. Add garlic and continue cooking for another minute.

6. Whisk eggs in a medium bowl, then add spinach, cooked onion, feta, salt, nutmeg and pepper and mix well.

Using Puff Pastry:

1. Place an unfolded, round sheet of puff pastry on the parchment paper and apply the spinach mixture over the pastry.

2. Keep it flat and fold them and seal them with a fork on the edges.

3. Take some egg wash and apply using a brush the top and the edges.

4. Make a few slits on the top and then bake for 40 minutes or until golden

brown and serve.

Using Filo Pastry:

1. If you would like to use filo pastry, use the folding pattern below. Fold two sheets of filo pastry in half so you get four individual layers.

2. Brush the strip of filo you just prepared with egg wash.

3. Drop some of the spinach mixture at the start and begin to fold over using the pattern below.

4. Top them with some sesame if you like before you bake.

Mmm. Opa!

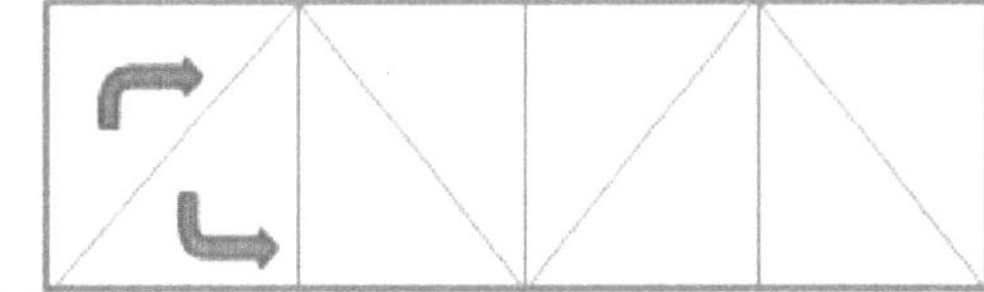

Sikotakia Tiganita

Makes 5-6 Servings

Ingredients

- 1 green bell pepper
- ½ onion
- 1 lb. chicken livers
- 1 oz. red wine
- Olive oil (for frying)

Directions:

1. Place livers on a towel to remove the excess moisture.
2. Once dry place in a bowl with oil and garlic.
3. Prepare a frying pan by adding oil and place liver chunks in the oil while when hot, be careful not to add the livers when the oil is too hot or they will pop very hot oil around. The same thing will happen when if is too cold because they will not sear initially, this will let them cook on contact with metal and they will stick to the pan.
4. Add some onion, green pepper, tomato and red wine for flavor.
5. Move the liver around in the pan often so it doesn't stick otherwise it

will pop and spray hot oil. Ideally, a non-stick pan helps greatly in making these.

6. Once the livers are firm all the way through remove them from the pan and place in a plate with some of the oil.

7. Garnish with some cold vegetables in a small bowl and serve with a side of tzatziki. Opa!

Avgolemono

Makes 4 servings

Ingredients

- 1 1/2 cups uncooked rice (brown or white basmati) 

- 8 chicken drumsticks

- 4 cups of chicken broth or

- 4 cups of water

- Salt to taste (approx. 2 tablespoons)

- Pepper to taste

- 1 whole lemon

- 2-3 eggs

Directions:

1. Take a large pot and boil all the chicken whole for 20-30 minutes.
2. After the chicken is done take the chicken out, drain the broth of the

chicken with the strainer into another pot.

3. Begin to boil the broth again.

4. During this time pull the chicken into small pieces and place into the boiling broth.

5. Add the rice and two more cups of water.

6. In a bowl, vigorously whisk/beat the eggs until they are frothy.

7. When the rice is finished in approximately 10 minutes place the broth that includes the rice and chicken slowly into the bowl with the egg while stirring.

8. Do not add the broth too fast or the egg will cook and clump rather than disperse within the soup making a creamy mixture.

9. Whisk as you add each scoop of broth. When ¾ of the broth is whisked into the bowl, place the mixture back into the pot.

10. Juice the lemon and whisk it into the pot with the rest of the soup.

11. Add salt and pepper to taste.

12. Serve and eat hot! Great for the Flu! Opa!

Fakies

Makes 4 servings

Ingredients

- 2 bay leaves
-
- 1 tablespoon of garlic, minced or sliced very thin
- 1/4 cup of olive oil
- 1 finely minced onion
- 1 finely chopped large carrot
- A pinch of dried oregano
- 1-tablespoon of tomato paste
- 1 pinch of rosemary (crushed and dried)
- Salt and black pepper (ground) to taste
- 1 teaspoon of red wine vinegar
- 1 teaspoon olive oil, or to taste
- 1 cup of brown lentils

Figure 1: Brown lentils

Directions

1. Place brown lentils (see Figure 1: Brown lentils) on a large open flat surface preferably a solid white counter. When you buy lentils from

your local organic market they will often have small stones among them you will have to look through them individually and pick out all the offenders. It sounds tedious and it can be but if you do it in small chunks of about 50-100 lentils at a time you should be done in about 5 minutes. You will not be able to separate the stones by throwing the peas in water or by sifting looking through them is the fastest way to do this and biting into a stone isn't a great way to impress guests or your dentist with newly acquired skill at cooking great Greek food.

2. Place the "safe" lentils in a large pot, add water, bring to a boil and cook for 10-15 minutes then drain and rinse.

3. Pour away the water. Heat olive oil in a saucepan over medium heat.

4. Add the carrot, onion and garlic and then cook until onion has cooked thoroughly.

5. Add the lentils, 1-quart water, bay leaves and rosemary then bring to boil.

6. Lower the heat to medium low.

7. Cover and simmer then add tomato paste, pepper, and salt (to taste) and then stir.

8. Simmer for 10 minutes then add water if the soup becomes too thick.

9. Serve and drizzle with olive oil, and/or red wine vinegar as desired and enjoy. Opa!

Fassolada

Makes 5 servings

Ingredients

- ½ cup of extra virgin olive oil

- 500g of white navy beans (dry)

- 1 chopped large red onion

- 2-3 chopped carrots

- 3 stalks of chopped celery

- 2-tablespoonof tomato paste

- Freshly ground pepper

Directions:

1. Put the beans in a saucepan.

2. Add cold water to cover them and bring to boil.

3. Reduce the heat and cook for 30-35 minutes making sure the beans are soft. Then strain in a colander once cooked.

4. Finely chop the celery, onion and carrots, add 3-4 tablespoons of olive oil in a deep pan, and then add the chopped vegetables and cook for about 2 minutes add some water if needed to keep anything from burning.

5. Lastly add the tomato paste.

6. Add the boiled beans in the pan then pour in enough boiling water to cover the beans, place the lid on and simmer for about 35 minutes.

7. Pour in the remaining olive oil, season with pepper and salt and boil until the soup becomes thick.

8. Serve with bread and add some black pepper. Opa!

Fava

Makes 6 Servings

Ingredients

- 75 grams of finely chopped onions
- 225 grams of yellow split peas
- 1 small crushed clove garlic
- 1-teaspoon of olive oil
- Lemon juice of half a lemon
- Salt and black pepper to taste

Directions:

1. Rinse split peas thoroughly and place them in a large saucepan with the onions and enough water to cover.

2. Bring to boil, reduce heat and simmer for 30-45 minutes in low heat until the split peas are thick.

3. Drain off excess water then place them in a bowl.

4. Beat in the lemon juice, garlic and oil until thick and well blended.

5. Let this cool and then add salt and pepper to taste.

Pat yourself on the back for a job well done, have a seat and eat. Opa!

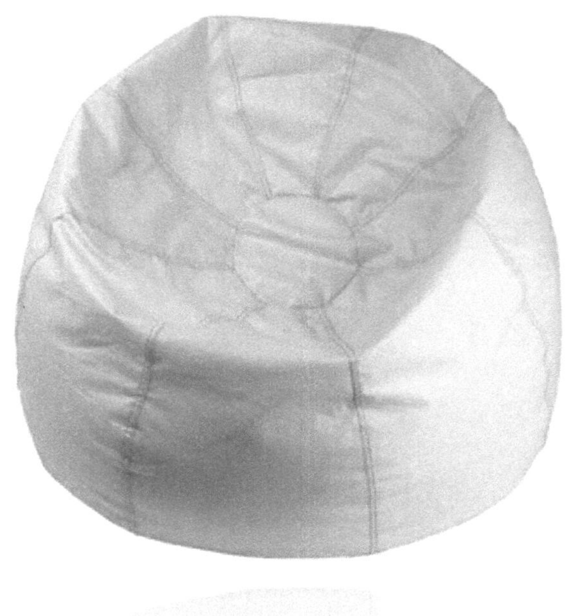

Keftedakia

Makes 6 servings

Ingredients:

- ½ pound of ground pork
- 1-pound of ground beef
- 2 minced garlic cloves
- 1 finely minced large onion
- Salt and pepper to taste
- 1/2 teaspoon of oregano (dry)
- 1/4 cup of milk
- 2 slices of no crusts white bread
- Oil (for frying)
- 1 whole egg
- Flour (for dredging)

Directions:

1. Combine onion, meat, salt, garlic, pepper and oregano in a bowl.

2. Take the bread crumbs and place them in the bowl. The reason for using bread crumbs is to make the meat bind together when cooking.

3. Combine meat, egg and bread then knead the mixture.

4. Make sure the mixture is even and then refrigerate for an hour.

5. Shape into balls, dredge in flour and sauté in hot oil then serve.

These can also be used as meatballs for spaghetti; they can be shaped into patties and made into burgers or shredded to make delicious gyros. Opa!

Dolmathes

Makes 4 servings

Ingredients

- 24 Grape vine leaves (come in a jar)

- 2 cups Basmati rice

- 1 spoonful of butter for the rice

- 1 pound Ground beef

- 2 ounces of Olive oil

- 1 Onion finely chopped

- 1 pinch of Salt and Pepper

- Oregano

- Parsley

- Basil

Directions:

1. Boil the rice (the rule is one part rice to three parts water).

2. Place 3 cups of water in a pot with the rice and the butter and cook for 8 minutes covered with a lid.

3. Put the rice in a container when it is finished.

4. Cut up the onions into small pieces and place into a pot with the olive oil.

5. Sautee the onions until they are cooked through then add the beef with chopped up chili, a pinch of oregano, parsley, and basil.

6. When cooked, mix the ground beef with the rice.

7. Lay one layer of leaves at the bottom of the pot with a small amount of oil on it.

8. Lay one leaf at a time down on a counter. Place one or 1-2 spoonful of rice in the area near the stem of the leaf the fold the "wings" of the leaf inward and roll toward the tip when folded place it in the pot.

9. When you have enough dolmathes prepared and you have a layer of dolmathes at the base of the pot, lay down another layer of leaves to

separate the upper layers from the lower layers. This will also help keep the dolmathes together when you simmer them later.

10. When you're all done, place a small plate over top of the dolmathes to hold them down while simmering.

11. Pour enough water into the pot to submerge the plate and place the pot on low heat. Simmer for 45 minutes.

12. When done drain off the water and then remove the plate from the top of the dolmathes and serve. Opa!

Saganaki

Makes 4 servings

Ingredients

- 8 rounds of grilled and quartered pita bread (brushed with olive oil)
- 8 Kefalogaviera cheese slices 1cm thick
- 1 cup of flour
- 2 cups of brandy (optional)
- Lemon juice (of 2 lemons)
- Enough milk to wet the cheese

Directions:

1. Prepare a lemon by placing it in hot water with the skin intact for 5 min.

2. Place two bowls next to each other: one for milk and another for flour.

3. Cut the cheese into slices 1 cm thick but at least 15cm long by 10cm wide.

4. Prepare a frying pan with generous amounts of oil, enough to submerge the cheese slice but leave the top above the oil.

5. Heat the oil to frying temperature. Make sure you cook one cheese slice at a time. There is not enough heat from a conventional stove top to cook two pieces at one time.

6. Dip the cheese slices into the milk first and then place it into the flour covering the entire surface. This is important! It must be covered evenly with flour.

7. Using tongs (due to the hot oil) gently place the cheese into the oil cooking only the one side for now.

8. Let it cook for 10 seconds at high temperature then lower the heat 20% and move it gently so it does not stick to the pan.

9. Let it brown just like in the picture above then flip it over and repeat on the other side.

10. After you flip it, break open the hard skin that has formed from frying it so that you can later drop the lemon juice inside.

11. When the cheese forms a skin on the bottom, use tongs or a fork and pick at the edges to force a crust to form there. The broken and hardened cheese crust will hold the oil and lemon juice later.

12. Check on the lemon, if it's warm and you are confident it is warm throughout cut it in half.

13. Check the cheese for color one last time then turn the heat on full and let the oil get hotter. Take the pan and have another pan to transfer the hot oil to leaving only a little oil with the cheese.

14. Be careful on this next part, take the lemon and squeeze it onto the cheese quickly. You will only have half a second before the pan rejects the lemon juice and explodes into a fireball (see below). Drop the lemon

into the pan face down when it's safe.

15. You can cook the inside of the lemon for a few seconds and remove the pan from the heat. If possible serve the saganaki in the pan on a hotplate. Accompany it with a few slices of pita bread for dipping the lemon juice and oil.

Don't burn yourself or set anything on fire! Dropping lemon in the oil will easily make a fireball that will hit the ceiling and anything flammable on the wall. We suggest you do this part outside or away from open flames which could ignite the air/oil mixture. It is the only way to make this dish very delicious instead of just ok. Opa!

Pastitsio

Makes 4 Servings

Ingredients

- 4-ounce of mushrooms (optional)

- 4 ounces olive oil

- 1 1/2 pound of ground beef

- 1 finely chopped small onion

- 2 finely chopped cloves of garlic

- 8 - 12 ounces of tomato paste

- 1/4 cup of parmesan cheese

- Salt and pepper

-

  a1/4 teaspoon of nutmeg

- 1/4 teaspoon of cinnamon

- 1 egg yolk

- 1/4 cups of butter

- 2 liters of milk

- 8 tablespoon scoops of cornstarch

- 2 cups of macaroni preferably extruded with ribs (cooked)

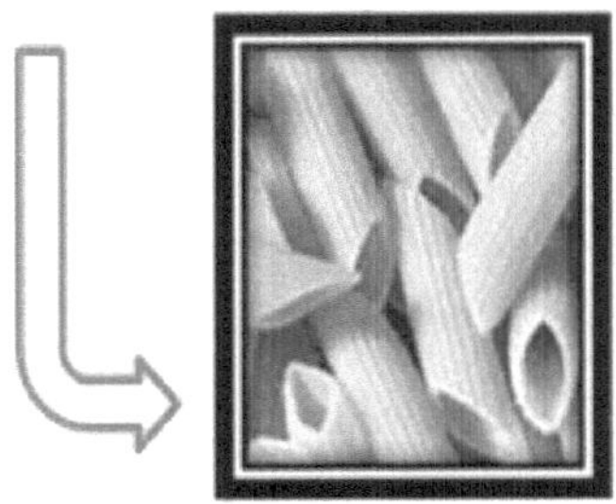

Directions:

1. Boil the macaroni is a large pot with a small amount of oil and a pinch of salt.

2. After the macaroni is boiled take it out of the pot and place it aside in a strainer.

3. Afterwards, you must sauté the onions and garlic in the pot with the oil until they just start to brown on the edge.

4. Add the ground beef into the pot and then add pepper, salt and tomato paste. Cook for 5 to 10 minutes while stirring on medium to high heat.

5. Put half the macaroni in a pan and cover with a layer of the ground beef.

6. Combine the nutmeg, cinnamon and parmesan cheese then sprinkle over meat and top with macaroni.

7. Clean the pot you just used by scrubbing with soap and water to make sure there is no oil left over from cooking the meat as this could curdle the milk in the next step.

8. Take a small bowl and add about 50ml of cold milk.

9. Scoop out 8 tablespoons of cornstarch and whisk until dissolved (note: cornstarch does not dissolve in hot liquids do this step with cold milk.)

10. Place the pot on the stove set the heat from high to medium and add the milk to the pot.

11. Take a wooden spoon and stir the pot continuously while the milk heats up.

12. When the milk just starts to emit steam add the milk with the corn starch and use the whisk to mix.

13. When the milk starts to thicken add butter and stir to melt and blend completely.

14. Add one egg yolk and a pinch of salt to the milk and whisk to blend.

15. Pour over beef and macaroni and bake for 20-40 minutes in the oven at 175C (350F) until it is golden brown.

You can also substitute the instructions below to make traditional béchamel sauce. In this recipe we used corn starch as it is easier to complete the dish using this method. If you want to go with the harder traditional recipe for the white béchamel, see below:

To make the béchamel sauce:

1. Put milk in a saucepan and stir while heating.

2. Melt the butter in a large skillet over medium heat then lower the heat.

3. Whisk in flour and pour into the hot milk very slowly.

4. Whisk constantly until it thickens.

5. At the end, you will have to season with a pinch of salt, nutmeg, and white pepper. Opa!

Mousaka

Make 3 servings

Ingredients

4 ounce can of tomato paste

- 3 eggplants (thick lengthwise slices)
- 1-tablespoon of butter
- ¼ cup of olive oil
- Ground black pepper
- 1 pound of ground lean beef
- Salt to taste
- 2 finely chopped onions
- 1 beaten egg
- 1/4 teaspoon of ground cinnamon
- 1 minced clove garlic
- 1/4 teaspoon of ground nutmeg
- 1/2 cups of parmesan cheese
- 2 tablespoons of parsley (dried)
- 1/2 cup of red wine
- 4 cups of milk
- 6 tablespoons flour
- 1/2 cup of butter for béchamel
- Ground white pepper

Directions:

1. Place slices of eggplant on paper towels, sprinkle some salt and set aside for 30 minutes.

2. Heat the olive oil in a skillet and fry the eggplant until browned then set aside on paper towels to drain.

3. In a large skillet over medium heat, melt the butter, add the onions, garlic, salt and pepper along with ground beef.

4. Sprinkle parsley, nutmeg and herbs and pour in the tomato sauce with some wine.

5. Simmer for 20 minutes, allow it to cool and stir in beaten egg.

6. To make the béchamel sauce: Put milk in a saucepan and stir while heating.

7. Melt the butter in a large skillet over medium heat then lower the heat.

8. Whisk in flour and pour into the hot milk very slowly.

9. Whisk constantly until it thickens.

10. At the end, you will have to season with a pinch of salt, nutmeg, and white pepper.

11. Place a layer of eggplant in a greased baking dish then cover eggplant with meat mixture.

12. Add ½ cup of Parmesan cheese and cover with remaining eggplant.

13. Add another ½ cup of cheese on top then pour the béchamel sauce over the top and garnish with nutmeg and the remaining cheese.

14. Bake for an hour then serve hot. Opa!

Psomi (Greek bread)

Makes 2 Servings

Ingredients:

- 1-tablespoon of semolina

- 6 cups of all-purpose flour

- 2 cups of water

- 1 dry yeast (envelope active)

- 3 teaspoons of sugar

- 2 teaspoons of salt

- 1 tablespoon of butter (melted)

Directions:

1. Pour flour into a mixing bowl and place into a low heat oven to warm.
2. Put the yeast in ½ cup warm water and pour in remaining water, sugar, and salt.
3. Take out flour from oven then take 2 cups of flour from the bowl and put aside.
4. Pour in the liquid in the remaining flour and put in a little of the flour until the liquid gets thick.
5. Cover the bowl and leave in a warm place until the mixture is frothy.
6. Stir the rest of the flour, add the butter and beat with a wooden spoon until smooth.
7. Sprinkle a little flour onto a board, and turn the dough out.
8. Combine some of the flour (that was kept aside) and knead in a small quantity to keep the dough from sticking and then shape into a ball.
9. Oil the dough and put it in a bowl, cover with plastic and allow to rise in a warm place for 2 hours.
10. Press down and make into 2 pieces then shape into torpedoes.
11. Grease baking sheet, put the dough well apart on the sheet, cut four diagonal slashes across the dough and allow the dough to proof by covering with a moist cloth.
12. Preheat oven to 375 degrees F.
13. Put a dish of boiling water on the bottom of the oven.
14. Take a mister, spray bread lightly and bake in preheated oven for 40 minutes.
15. Take out, let cool and serve. Opa!

Thank you, *please leave a review!*

We thank you for purchasing our book. We would appreciate from the bottom of our hearts if you could please leave a review. Opa!

Homemade food is delicious and please don't be selfish share plenty with your friends with a glass of wine or two… don't be gluttonous. Enjoy.